christopher Kazoo & Bongo Boo

Written by R.O. Price • Illustrated by Nancy Coffelt

Little School House Books™ • Los Angeles

Story concept by R.O. Price & John Henry Kreitler
Art Direction by Lynne Versaw Creative Services
Book Layout by Stuart Silverstein, stuartsilversteindesign

Audio Version:
Story read by Kathryn Skatula
Music by John Henry Kreitler
Songs by John Henry Kreitler, Patsy Meyer, Tyana Parr & Susan Kay Wyatt

ISBN : 978-0-9798845-0-4
Library of Congress Control No: 2007935720
Printed in the USA. First printing, February 2008

The Illustrations in this book were created using oil pastels on black paper.

Little School House Books • Los Angeles
www.littleschoolhousebooks.com

To Shane, Steve, Johnny, Kevin and Treezie — RP

For Lynne – a steady soul and a good heart— NC

Christopher and Boo were best friends. They lived next door to each other in a big apartment building on K Street.

Every morning after breakfast, Christopher and Boo played in the garden behind their building. Sometimes they played games like hide-and-seek. Sometimes they taught tricks to Christopher's dog, Freckles.

One sunny summer morning, Boo came outside with something new to do. She was carrying what looked like two little drums tied together.

"What's that?" Christopher asked her.

Boo grinned. "They're bongos!"

"Bongos?" Christopher said. "What are bongos?"

"I'll **show you**," Boo said. She put the bongos between her knees and firmly slapped the tops of the little drums. The sounds she made were wonderful! There was a **bong-bong-bong** and a **cong-cong-cong**, then a **bong** and a **cong** and a **bong-cong-bong**.

Before long, Freckles stood on his hind legs and began to jump up and down. Then Mac the macaw flew down from the window sill of Apartment 3-C and started whistling. Soon after that, Christopher's friend, Shayla, ran outside and began to sing and dance.

Everybody was having a great time! Everybody, that is, except for Christopher. He was feeling a little left out, and maybe a teensy weensy bit jealous. The truth was he wished he had bongos like Boo.

Boo could see how Christopher felt and was ready to share her bongos with him. But before she could, there suddenly came a loud thrashing from the trees at the back of the yard.

Out jumped Tang the orangutan!

"Helllllooooooooooo!" Tang howled, startling everyone.

Tang was Christopher's most mysterious friend. Nobody knew where he came from or where he lived, and although he was very friendly, he had a very bad habit. He stole things. Tang was a thief.

"Hi, Tang," Christopher said. "It's nice to see you, but I hope you don't plan to steal Boo's new bongos."

"Nooooooooo," howled Tang. Then the orangutan reached into the colorful bag hanging from his neck.

"For yooouuuuuuu," he howled at Christopher.

Tang handed Christopher what looked like a tiny submarine with round holes at both ends. On either side of it, a beautiful silver star glittered in the sun. **"What is this?"** Christopher asked.

"It's a kazoo!" said Boo, who knew about such things.
"He's giving you a present so you can make music too.
All you have to do is hum into it."

Christopher threw Tang a suspicious look. "Thank you, Tang,"
he said, "but are you sure you didn't steal this?"

The orangutan fluttered his lips as if to say, **"Don't be silly."**
Then he jumped back in the trees and disappeared.

"Come on, Christopher," Boo said. "Play your kazoo."

"No," Christopher said. "It's **wrong. This isn't mine. Tang stole this, I just know it.**"

Christopher's friends were disappointed. Freckles whined sadly, Shayla sighed wearily, and Mac let out a long, mournful whistle.

"Awww, please, Christopher," Boo said. "**Just play it for a little while. Then you can give it back.**"

Christopher still didn't think he should, but he finally gave in. **"Well, okay, just for a little while,"** he said, and he lifted the kazoo to his lips. Everyone was quiet as a mouse as he hummed into it. Out came a wonderful sound.

"**Wow!**" he marveled. "**This is great!**" He and Boo began playing together, and the whole garden turned into a party. Freckles started jumping again, Shayla sang her song and danced, and Mac flapped his wings and whistled. Even Squeeze, the snake who lived in the bushes, enjoyed it.

But then it happened. As Christopher played his kazoo, he hit a very high note. Suddenly, a shower of stars burst from the kazoo and instantly all his friends froze like statues. They were completely still. Not so much as an eye was blinking or a pinkie finger stirring.

"Oh no!" Christopher wailed. "What's happened to everyone?" He raced from one friend to the next, waving his hands in their faces and trying to shake them out of their deep freeze. But they didn't so much as quiver.

Frantic, Christopher ran into the apartment building and grabbed his friend, Moon Ji.

"**What should I do?**" Christopher asked him.

After Moon Ji studied the matter, he shook his head. "**I think you'd better tell your mother,**" he said. So that's what Christopher did.

As soon as his startled mother saw the frozen figures in the garden, she raced to the telephone and called the police.

When two police officers arrived, both scratched their heads. **"Darndest thing I ever saw,"** said the first officer.

"Exactly what were you doing when this happened?" the other one asked Christopher.

So Christopher showed them, but when he hit that same high note on his kazoo — **Presto!** Out flew more stars, and just like that, the two officers and Moon Ji all froze too!!

"Oh my goodness!!" cried Christopher. "This is terrible. I never, never, never should have used something that didn't belong to me!"

Suddenly a voice behind him screeched, **"That's right little boy! Look what you've done!"** Christopher whirled around. Standing by the fence was the strangest woman he had ever seen. She wore a long black dress and a wrinkled black hat, all of it sprinkled with silver stars like the ones on the kazoo. She was waving a star-studded black cane at Christopher, and she looked very mad!

"That's my kazoo!!!" the woman shouted.

"I'm sorry," Christopher said. "I really am. I was going to give it back. I didn't steal it."

"Oh, I know who stole it," the woman said. "It was that miserable pet of mine, the orangutan."

"Tang is YOUR orangutan?" Christopher said.

"I should turn him into a mouse," she replied, "and maybe
I should turn YOU into a mouse, or a rabbit, or a pig,
for using someone else's kazoo. You should know better."

Christopher gulped. "Are you a wi-wi-witch?" he asked nervously.

"My name is Madame Starr," the strange woman said. "Now give
me back my kazoo at once!"

Christopher quickly handed it over. But then an amazing thing happened. The kazoo flew out of the woman's grasp and zoomed right back into Christopher's hand!

Madame Starr looked shocked. **"That kazoo certainly has a mind of its own,"** she grumbled to Christopher. **"Well, if it likes you so much, you must be a good boy at heart. I guess that kazoo is yours to keep, child."** And with that, the woman started to hobble off.

"Wait!" Christopher called after her. "What about my friends? They're still frozen."

"Think opposites," Madame Starr said. "You froze them with the highest note. Just find the lowest note, and that will probably thaw them out." Then, just like that, Madame Starr disappeared in a shower of silver stars.

Christopher had no choice but to take her advice.
Putting his lips to the kazoo, he began to hum low notes.
He went lower and lower and lower.

When he hit the lowest note of all, everyone suddenly snapped out of the deep freeze! Strangely, though, no one seemed to know that anything unusual had happened. Boo went on playing her bongos, Mac whistled, and Shayla sang and danced.

Freckles fell down, but then he got right back up and kept jumping. To Christopher's surprise, even Moon Ji and the officers starting dancing. So Christopher hummed on his kazoo once more. But he made sure that he NEVER played the highest note again.

Later, after everyone else had left, Christopher told
Boo all about the deep freeze and Madame Starr. When
he finished the story, Boo looked very upset.

"What's wrong?" Christopher asked.

"I'm worried about my bongos," Boo said. "You see,
the truth is that … well … they were a present from Tang."

"Tang!" Christopher cried. "Oh, my gosh, Boo. Do you think they could be magic, too?"

At that very instant, the bongos did a **cong-bong-cong** all by themselves!! When Boo and Christopher's eyes grew almost as big as the bongos, the kazoo made a funny little noise that sounded a lot like a giggle.

From that day on, the two friends were known as the magical Christopher Kazoo and Bongo Boo.

THE END

MEET THE AUTHOR
Richard Owen Price has been writing and editing professionally since the age of nine. He spent many years with USA Today in roles ranging from staff correspondent to deputy managing editor and was nominated twice for a Pulitzer Prize. Price also contributes articles to a variety of magazines, specializing in celebrity interviews. A father of five, he particularly enjoys writing features about youngsters -- including his own -- an experience that he credits as the inspiration for his children's stories.

MEET THE ILLUSTRATOR
Nancy Coffelt has always loved art and writing, so when she grew up it was only natural she wanted to make a career in children's books. Nancy Coffelt lives and works in Portland, Oregon and draws and writes surrounded by her friends, family and a pack of bad, bad, wiener dogs. Her books include *Goodnight Sigmund*, *Dogs in Space* and *Fred Stays With Me*.